D1624841

For
GOD and
COUNTRY

Forty Great Hymns of
Joy and Celebration

Newport Classic, Ltd.
Providence, Rhode Island
1992

Published by:
Newport Classic, Ltd.
106 Putnam Street
Providence, Rhode Island 02909

ISBN 0-9632045-0-5

FOR GOD AND COUNTRY: Forty Great Hymns of Joy and Celebration
Text: Braider, Jackson N. (b. 1954)
Musical Arrangements: Newman, Anthony (b. 1941)
Catalogue information: Hymns/Music/Religion

SECOND PRINTING, MAY 1992

PRINTED IN THE UNITED STATES
BY R.I. LITHO PRINTING INC.

TABLE OF CONTENTS

About the Artists

Anthony Newman (organist and arranger) has, for the past 25 years, been America's premier performer of Bach as well as of Mozart and Beethoven. A church organist since his early teens, Mr. Newman most recently served as the Music Director of the Episcopal Church of the Holy Trinity in New York City. He has recorded over 120 albums for Columbia Masterworks, Deutsche Grammophon, Sony Classical, and Newport Classic. In 1987, he won *Stereo Review's* Record of the Year award for his recording of Beethoven's third piano concerto with the Philomusica Antiqua of London.

The Chestnut Brass Company have established themselves at the forefront of American brass ensemble playing, from their participation as soloists in the soundtrack of Ken Burns' historic *Civil War* documentary to their extraordinary renditions of mid-19th century masterpieces on *Listen to the Mockingbird*.

Jackson Braider (annotator), prior to joining the staff of Newport Classic in 1990, worked at both Random House and Delacorte Press in New York. A contributing editor of *Acoustic Guitar* magazine, he earned his degrees in music history and folklore and has been writing about music and musicians for 15 years. Mr. Braider was assistant director of the Nightwatch program at the Cathedral of St. John the Divine in New York from 1985 to 1991.

A Note about the Recording

In the compact disc accompanying this volume, Anthony Newman and the Chestnut Brass Company perform each of the hymns through three verses. The first verse features standard accompaniment, the second a descant highlighting the brass players, while the third verse is generally dedicated to bathing the listener in a wash of glorious liturgical sound.

Copies of the horn parts are available from:

Ellis Music Press
19 Fifth Street
East Norwalk, Connecticut 06855
Tel. 203-838-9651

Acknowledgments

Though *For God and Country* is the first hymnal to include recorded accompaniment and background information on the hymns, we have been following trails that have been clearly marked by hymnodists and authorities on sacred song since the turn of the century.

Thanks are due first to Larry and Shelley Kraman, who have persistently fought on behalf of the idea that compact discs and books can be combined to create something greater than the mere sum of the individual parts. I can only hope that this text merits the enthusiastic support they have given to this project from the very start.

I am particularly grateful to the editors of *The Harvard University Hymnbook* (1964) for the scholarship and insight of their encapsulated descriptions of the hymns contained in their text; if the number of footnotes can be a measure of gratitude, then, as the reader will see, I owe a great, great deal to *Veritas*.

I cannot say enough about the scrupulous attention paid by Arlene, Larry, Shelley, and Steve in the final preparation of the galleys. Newport Classic is a land where the people wear many hats—who would have thought that proofreading would be among them?

Last and certainly not least, my deepest thanks are due to Jennifer Lowe for her conscientious, meticulous, and astute work with the manuscript. Jenny has a rare brilliance that elevates the IQ of all around her. Her incisive comments and dedication to the word (in all its senses) all helped to make this a far better book than I could possibly have hoped for.

Jackson Braider,
Providence, Rhode Island
December 15, 1991

Credits:
Executive Producer: Lawrence J. Kraman
Producer and Engineer: Scott Johnson
Digital Editor: Stephen J. Epstein
Musical Arrangements: Anthony Newman
Cover Art and Design: Glenn Southwick
Text: Jackson Braider
Editor: Jennifer Lowe
Digital Mastering: Jonathan Wyner, Northeastern Digital Recording, Inc.
Recorded at: The Church of the Holy Trinity, New York City

Introduction

Ye watchers and ye holy ones,
Bright seraphs, cherubim, and thrones,
Raise the glad strain
Alleluia!

"Lasst Uns Erfreuen" (Cologne, 1623),
adapted by Athelstan Riley, 1906

I t is not unreasonable to ask what distinguishes the hymn from
any other type of song. Hymns are extremely powerful songs of
religious content, composed and sung by men and women over the
centuries as testimonies of faith, as demonstrations of belief, as expres-
sions of love for humankind as well as for God. Because they are
dedicated to the spiritual side of our nature, hymns give voice—quite
literally—to those feelings that might otherwise be stifled in our daily
lives: love, for example, and humility; faith; hope; courage. No other
form of human expression has touched on our concerns, as individuals
and as communities, the way hymns have; no body of song more fully
represents our needs, our hopes, and our joys as do the several hundred
hymns that form the core of the music ministry in churches today.

From this rich and extraordinary collection of text and melody,
Anthony Newman and the Chestnut Brass Company have culled the
forty hymns in our volume to celebrate the millions of people, now and
over the past 500 years, who have blended their voices and beliefs in
this great musical tradition.

When we look at them in light of their long history, hymns
provide an emotional continuum between past and present. Many of
these songs are songs that our grandparents and their parents before
them sang; many are deeply enmeshed in our own childhood Sunday
experiences. They serve as a living tradition that links us not only to
the church—be we Episcopalians or Lutherans, Baptists, Congregation-
alists, Methodists, Presbyterians or Catholics—but to what we all have
in common, our very humanity.

In this collection, we have drawn hymns from different ages,
different countries, and different faiths. Far from being a form which
focuses exclusively on the kingdom of heaven, the hymn can also

glorify communities of people in its role as a national song or anthem. Why have we chosen to include national hymns and songs from such diverse places as England, Austria, Saxony, Scotland, and Russia, as well as America?

This is an interesting question to raise in a country where we chose to establish a fundamental separation between church and state. Looking at our antecedents, we see how Europe's history through the eighteenth century—and even into the present day and age—was dominated by powerful religious groups (and all were to blame at various times) actively seeking to oppress those who differed from them. At the time, America was one of the few places where the persecuted had the right to pursue their own spiritual practices without fear of being disenfranchised, persecuted, or killed—if only because here, dissenters could always break off and found a new community in this continent's vast wilderness of three hundred years ago.

So by including national songs among our hymns, we are trying to look beyond the sentiments that have caused so much of this world's needless bloodshed—patriotism and religion in their basest forms. We want to show that, for happy and productive people everywhere, every land is its own *promised* land. And nationalism, in its healthiest expression, is comparable to the natural pride one takes in one's own home as a place of freedom and autonomy.

An interesting note to the reader is that, while each country became inspired to promote a sense of its own identity in song, the seed of that song often came from elsewhere. The Scottish national hymn, OLD 124TH (included here with the text, "Now Israel May Say, and That Truly"), was originally composed for the *Geneva Psalter* by a French Calvinist. England's "God Save Our Gracious King" inspired not only the Austrians and Russians to write their own national hymns, it provided the tune for national songs in both the United States and Saxony. We speak of "one nation under God," but if the derivation of national songs is anything to go by, we would probably do better to speak of "one world."

Beyond the matter of its content, much of the power of the hymn in our hearts and minds is derived from the fact that the hymn is sung by the congregation, the voices of many joined in a single utterance. To understand the history of the hymn, then, it is important to understand the history of congregational singing. And the beginning, in that sense, was the Reformation and the way in which Martin Luther revolutionized the role of the congregation in the act of worship.

Before Luther, the participation of the congregation was limited to spoken responses, practically always uttered in Latin, a language most people did not even speak or understand. Chanting and singing were restricted to the priests and the choir, acknowledged and trained participants in the liturgy. Scripture was faithfully transcribed in Latin and Greek; the Readings—the Old Testament, the Epistle, and the Gospel—were all in Latin. Only the educated could appreciate the words of St. Paul or understand the inspiration from which the priest drew his sermon. For the rest, the Mass was a testimony of unquestioning faith.

The decision to translate the Bible and other sacred texts into the vernacular was a profound revelation for the people of Northern Europe in the sixteenth century. There were no longer any secrets in the act of worship for the congregation. Where they had followed blindly, the members of the congregation were now obliged to develop their own appreciation and understanding of deeper moral truths.

At the start, congregational singing was restricted almost entirely to paraphrases of the Psalter—witness the early hymnbooks of Luther and Jean Calvin. Luther cites no less an authority than St. Paul in proclaiming that the singing of psalms and spiritual songs will help spread abroad "God's word and Christ's teaching." He continues,

> As a good beginning and to encourage those who can do better, I and several others have brought together certain spiritual songs with a view to spreading abroad and setting in motion the holy Gospel which now, by the grace of God, has again emerged...[1]

Through the judicious practice of paraphrasing texts and setting them to folk melodies already well known to members of the congregation, Luther and Calvin laid the foundation for a body of song that was both easy to remember and easy to sing. Singable, accessible, memorable: these became the watchwords for psalmody and hymnody as the practice for congregational composition developed, and they have informed the collation of hymnals ever since, whether it was in subse-

---

[1]Cited in Oliver Strunk, *Source Readings in Music History*, Vol. II, pps. 151-152.

quent editions of the *Wittemburg Gesangbuch* or the most recent edition
of the Episcopal hymnal, published in 1982.

Here, of course, we are concerned primarily with hymns in the
English-speaking world. And no history of English hymnody would be
complete without reference to Isaac Watts, a pastor to the Independent
congregation in Mark Lane, London, during the first half of the eighteenth century. Though frail of health, Watts wrote almost six hundred
different hymns and published numerous collections that were to
inspire hymn writers in the years to come. He often wrote paraphrases
of psalms and Scripture, but he also broke ground by authoring entirely
new spiritual texts, and it was here particularly that he provided the
model for future generations of English hymnodists, most notably the
Reverend Reginald Heber, whose collection, *Hymns written and adapted
to the weekly church service of the year* (1827), was by far the most popular
hymnal published in the first half of the nineteenth century.

Though there were great hymn writers prior to Heber—Isaac
Watts, Charles Wesley, Martin Luther, and many others—the true
acceptance of the hymn in the English service occurred with the publication of the first edition of *Hymns Ancient and Modern* in 1861. It was in
the preparation of this collection that we find the editors drawing
inspiration from a wide variety of sources: Catherine Winkworth's
seminal translation of the German Reformist literature; John Mason
Neale's work with the writings of the Early Church; the Calvinist
Geneva Psalter; hymn writers Congregationalist, Lutheran, Presbyterian,
Anglican, Baptist, and Catholic. Music flowed from America, Austria,
Croatia, Russia, Germany, France, Bohemia, the British Isles, and Italy.

Since then, a certain measure of standardization has taken place.
Readers will see that a number of texts, even in this small volume, have
more than one musical accompaniment. What is more, some tunes
have been used to accompany different texts. A hymn you may know
in one circumstance may be something entirely different for another
reader. In some cases, we have even gone so far as to write entirely
new texts. In this sense, we are together with the long tradition of
hymn editors for whom the hymn is not so much a matter of melody or
even of text; the important thing is the *singing*.

The instrumental recording by Anthony Newman and the Chestnut Brass Company ranges in mood from quiet and contemplative to triumphantly joyous; the only thing missing is the singing—which is for you to provide. That is why we have included the simple arrangements—some traditional, others by Mr. Newman—and words for these hymns, as well as some notes on their texts, composers, and inspirations. The sources of many of these great hymns may surprise you!

So we hope that you will take advantage of this opportunity—whether you are a teacher, chorus director, a member of a musical family, or just a shower-singer—to join in and "raise the glad strain" along with our recording. Even if you don't feel that you can carry a tune in a bucket, just remember what St. John Crysostom wrote to noviates in the fourth century:

> Here there is no need for art which is slowly perfected; there is need only for lofty purpose ... One may sing without voice, the words resounding in the mind. For we sing, not to men, but to God, who can hear our hearts and enter into the silence of our beings.[2]

---

[2]Cited in *Strunk*, Vol. 1, pg. 70.

No. 1: A Mighty Fortress Is Our God
originally *Ein' feste Burg ist unser Gott*

Music: **Martin Luther**; arr. and harm.: **Johann Sebastian Bach** (1685-1750)
Words: **Martin Luther** (1483-1546); trans.: **Frederic Henry Hedge** (1805-90)

Perhaps the most famous of all hymns attributed to Martin Luther, "A Mighty Fortress Is Our God" draws its inspiration from Psalm 46 ("God is our hope and strength: a very present help in trouble"). Among the early Lutherans (up to and including those of Bach's day), this hymn was typically associated with the Festival of the Reformation. Bach himself used it numerous times in his composition—most notably in two different cantatas devoted to the Festival of the Reformation.

The translator of this text, Frederic Henry Hedge, was a graduate of both Harvard College and Harvard Divinity School. Having served as a Unitarian minister in Maine, Rhode Island, and Massachusetts, Hedge returned to Harvard to teach ecclesiastical history and German literature.

In 1853, Hedge published *Hymns for the Church of Christ*, which he had edited with Frederic Dan Huntington. It was from this collection that the hymn as we know it today was taken.[1]

---

[1] See *Harvard University Hymn Book* (Cambridge, Mass.: 1964) , pg. 331. Also see Gunter Stiller, *Johann Sebastian Bach and Liturgical Life in Leipzig* (trans. Bouman, Poellet, and Oswald; St. Louis: 1984), pg. 239 and pg. 247.

No. 1: A Mighty Fortress Is Our God

Did we in our own strength confide, our striving would be losing
Were not the right man on our side, the man of God's own choosing
Dost ask who that may be? Christ Jesus it is he
Lord Sabaoth his Name, from age to age the same
And he must win the battle.

And though this world, with devils filled, should threaten to undo us
We will not fear, for God hath willed his truth to triumph through us
The prince of darkness grim, we tremble not for him
His rage we can endure, for lo! his doom is sure
One little word shall fell him.

No. 2: Praise to God, Immortal Praise

Music: Dix, melody **Conrad Kocher** (1786-1872); arr. **William Henry Monk** (1823-1889)

Words: **Anna Laetitia Barbauld** (1743-1825)

Anna Laetitia Barbauld counts among the women who contributed to the formation of English hymnody, like Catherine Winkworth, Margaret Barclay, and Frances Elizabeth Cox, to name a few. The wife of a Unitarian minister who had emigrated from France, Barbauld operated a boarding school in Suffolk.

"Praise to God, Immortal Praise" was first published in William Enfield's collection, *Hymns for Public Worship* (1772). When it was selected for publication in *Hymns Ancient and Modern*, William Henry Monk linked Barbauld's text with a melody he had used for another hymn, William Chatterton Dix's "As with gladness men of old" (see No. 40 below).

The original tune was by Conrad Kocher and was featured in the collection *Stimmen aus dem Reiche Gottes* (1838), where it was set to the text, "Treuer Heiland, wir sind hier." (For William Henry Monk, see No. 4, "The Strife Is O'er"; for Conrad Kocher, see No. 20, "Holy God, We Praise Thy Name")[2]

Typically, this hymn is sung in conjunction with Thanksgiving Day in the United States.

---

[2] See *Harvard,* pg. 300 and pg. 304.

No. 2: Praise to God, Immortal Praise

Praise to God, im-mor-tal praise, for the love that crowns our days; boun-teous
source of ev-ery joy, let thy praise our tongues em-ploy; all to
thee, our God, we owe, source whence all our bless-ings flow.

All the plenty summer pours; autumn's rich o'erflowing stores;
flocks that whiten all the plain; yellow sheaves of ripened grain:
Lord, for these our souls shall raise
grateful vows and solemn praise.

As thy prospering hand hath blessed, may we give thee of our best;
and by deeds of kindly love for thy mercies grateful prove;
singing thus through all our days
praise to God, immortal praise.

No. 3: Jesus Christ Is Risen Today

Music: Easter Hymn, from *Lyra Davidica* (1708)
Words: St. 1: "Surrexit Christus hodie" (14th cent.)
  Sts. 2, 3: *The Compleat Psalmodist*, ed. **John Arnold** (1749-50)
  St. 4: **Charles Wesley** (1740-88)

Believed to have originated in Bohemia, the first verse of this celebrated Easter hymn was written in Latin in the 1300s. The text was translated and set to the Easter Hymn in the *Lyra Davidica* ("David's Lyre"), published in London in 1708. The *Lyra* counted among the first English hymnals intended to replace the kind of psalmic paraphrases that described the congregational participation in the Anglican church of seventeenth century.

In 1750, John Arnold replaced the original verses two and three with words of his own and arranged the melody as we know it today. Charles Wesley, called the poet of the Methodist movement,[3] composed his single-stanza "Hymn to the Trinity" in 1740. This verse was subsequently added as a "doxology"—a closing phrase—to the hymn.

The result is a truly ecumenical work, drawing from medieval, Anglican, and Methodist traditions.

---

[3] See *Harvard*, pg. 294 and pg. 312.

No. 3: Jesus Christ Is Risen Today

Je- sus Christ is risen to- day Al- le- lu- ia!

Our tri- um- phant ho- ly day Al- le- lu- ia!

who did once up- on the cross, Al- le- lu- ia!

suf- fer to re- deem our loss Al- le- lu- ia!

Hymns of praise then let us sing, Alleluia!
unto Christ, our heavenly King, Alleluia!
who endured the cross and grave, Alleluia!
sinners to redeem and save, Alleluia!

But the pains which he endured, Alleluia!
our salvation have procured, Alleluia!
now above the sky he's King, Alleluia!
where the angels ever sing. Alleluia!

Sing we to our God above, Alleluia!
praise eternal as his love, Alleluia!
praise him, all ye heavenly host, Alleluia!
Father, Son, and Holy Ghost. Alleluia!

No. 4: The Strife Is O'er

Music: Victory, **Giovanni Pierluigi da Palestrina** (16th cent. Ital.);
     adapt. and arr.: **William Henry Monk** (1823-89)
Words: Latin, 1695; trans. **Francis Pott** (1832-1909)

Giovanni Pierluigi da Palestrina was an organist, singer, composer, and master of the Julian Chapel, serving both Popes Julius III and Paul IV at the Sistine Chapel, St. Peter's, and a number of other Roman churches. Through his powerful position as musician to the Popes, Palestrina was able to codify the rules of counterpoint. In particular, he recognized that the manner in which various musical lines interacted was every bit as important as the nature of the individual parts themselves.

William Henry Monk was organist and choirmaster of King's College at the University of London in the mid-nineteenth century. A major contributor to *Hymns Ancient and Modern*, the first major collection of Anglican hymns, Monk was one of the figures who determined the distinctive style of the Episcopalian "sound" as we know it today.

That having been said, "The Strife Is O'er" is quite different from the majority of hymns in its use of triple as opposed to duple time. While triple time is generally waltz-like, the feeling here, especially in the "Alleluia" antiphon with which the hymn opens and closes, is extremely unusual.

This is one of the few post-Reformation Catholic works that have passed into the Protestant hymn tradition.

No. 4: The Strife Is O'er

The powers of death have done their worst,
but Christ their legions hath dispersed:
let shout of holy joy outburst
Alleluia!

The three sad days are quickly sped,
he rises glorious from the dead:
all glory to our risen Head!
Alleluia!

(Repeat Antiphon)

No. 5: Lift Up Your Hearts
originally *Good Christians All, Rejoice and Sing!*

Music: Gelobt sei Gott, **Melchior Vulpius** (German, 1560?-1616)
Words: **Jackson Braider** (b. 1954)

Melchior Vulpius was a Lutheran Cantor in Weimar and is perhaps best known for his collection *Ein schön geistlich Gesangbuch*, published in Jena in 1609. It is from this Lutheran collection that the tune for "Lift Up Your Hearts" was taken.

As noted in the case of "The Strife Is O'er" (No. 4) hymns often change as they pass among differing traditions. Rather than translating the original text, authors sometimes choose to create an entirely new lyric for the hymn. Others, as in the instance of "Come, Ye Faithful, Raise the Strain" (No. 6), decide to set the translation of an older lyric to a more contemporary tune.

Here, we have set a new text to the tune by Vulpius, following Cyril A. Alington's example by focusing on the Resurrection. Many lay singers will note that the tune is that of "Good Christians All, Rejoice and Sing," which first appeared in the Episcopalian hymnody in the 1982 edition of the Hymnbook.

The tune itself is rather unusual in hymnody in its use of 6/4 time, a meter that combines duple beats with triple subdivisions.

No. 5: Lift Up Your Hearts

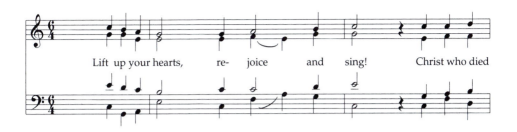

Lift up your hearts, re- joice and sing! Christ who died

re- turns as our King! All the great bells with joy we

ring: Al- le- lu- ia, al- le- lu- ia, al- le- lu- ia!

Christ the Lord is risen today
Behold the life, the empty grave
Raise your voices, rejoice and say
Alleluia!

The battle's done, the victory near
The chain is broke that bound our fear
The foe in flight our song they hear
Alleluia!

No. 6: Come, Ye Faithful, Raise the Strain

Music: St. Kevin, **Arthur Seymour Sullivan** (1842-1900)
Words: **St. John of Damascus** (*c.*696-*c.*754); trans. **Rev. John Mason Neale** (1818-66)

In the course of the nineteenth century, the Anglican church reconsidered and redefined the very nature of its hymnal. As the reader will note time and again in this volume, composers and arrangers during the period sought inspiration from a wide variety of sources—the fathers of the early church, the founders of the Reformation, composers and writers of their own time, or the psalmodists of the Catholic Church.

John Mason Neale, for most of his life a warden of Sackville College, a home for indigent old men located in South London, translated and adapted more than two hundred Greek and Latin texts, bringing the hymnody of the early and medieval church into the mainstream of the Anglican tradition.[4] A century and a half later, some fifty of Neale's translations are still included in the Episcopal hymnal.

The text, a translation of the Greek hymn that serves as the first ode of the Canon for Morning Prayer on the first Sunday after Easter in the Greek Orthodox liturgy, was set to the music of Arthur Seymour Sullivan of Gilbert and Sullivan fame.

This pairing of an eighth-century cleric, St. John of Damascus, and a nineteenth-century English composer best known for his humorous light opera may seem strange at first, but it is a wonderful example of the kind of cross-fertilization that characterizes much of modern hymnody .

[4] See *Harvard*, pg. 302.

No. 6: COME, YE FAITHFUL, RAISE THE STRAIN

Come, ye faith-ful, raise the strain of tri- um- phant glad- ness!
God hath brought his Is- ra- el in- to joy from sad- ness:
loosed from Pha-roah's bit- ter yoke Ja- cob's sons and daugh- ters,
led them with un- mois-tened foot through the Red Sea wa- ters.

'Tis the spring of souls today: Christ hath burst his prison
and from three days' sleep in death, a sun hath risen;
all the winter of our sins, long and dark is flying
from his light, to whom we give laud and praise undying.

Neither might the gates of death, nor the tomb's dark portal,
nor the watchers, nor the seal hold thee as a mortal:
but today amidst thine own thou didst stand, bestowing
that thy peace which evermore passeth human knowing.

No. 7: HE IS RISEN! HE IS RISEN!

Music: UNSER HERRSCHER, **Joachim Neander** (1650-1680)
Words: **Cecil Frances Alexander** (1818-1895)

Joachim Neander was rector of the Latin School at Düsseldorf and a leading proponent of music in the later Reformation. Both a poet and a musician, he published, in the last year of his life, a collection of works entitled *A und Ω. Joachimi Neandri Glaub- und Liebesübung* (Bremen, 1680). Several of these hymns were later translated for English congregations by Catherine Winkworth (see No. 10, "Sleepers, Awake!") and published in *The Chorale Book for England* (London, 1863).

UNSER HERRSCHER first appeared in Neander's own collection set to the hymn, "Unser Herrscher, unser König." John Mason Neale (see No. 6, "Come, Ye Faithful, Raise the Strain") first incorporated the tune in his collection *Medieval Hymns and Sequences* (1851).

Cecil Frances Alexander was the wife of the Archbishop of Armagh in Ulster. One of many hymn writers influenced by the Oxford Movement, she first published this text "He Is Risen! He Is Risen!" in 1846. Along with her many contributions to the hymnals, Cecil Frances Alexander was noted for her children's poetry. Her first volume of published work was "Hymns for Little Children" in 1847. Since then, over seventy different editions of this work have appeared in print.

Among her other famous hymns are "Once in royal David's city" and "All things bright and beautiful."[5]

---

[5]Harvey Blair Marks, *The rise and growth of English hymnody*, pps. 156-158.

No. 7: HE IS RISEN! HE IS RISEN!

He is ri-sen, he is ri-sen! Tell it out with joy-ful voice:

he has burst his three days' pri-son; let the whole wide earth re-joice:

death is con-quered, man is free, Christ has won the vic-to-ry.

Come, ye sad and fearful hearted, with glad smile and radiant brow!
Death's long shadows have departed; Jesus' woes are over now
and the passion that he bore—sin and pain can vex no more

Come, with high and holy hymning, hail our Lord's triumphant day;
not one darksome cloud is dimming yonder glorious morning ray,
breaking o'er the purple east, symbol of our Easter feast.

He is risen, he is risen! He hath opened heaven's gate:
we are free from sin's dark prison, risen to a holier state;
and a brighter Easter beam on our longing eyes shall stream.

No. 8: Behold the King
originally *Blest Be the King*

Music: **Melchior Teschner** (1584-1635)
Words: **Jackson Braider** (b. 1954)

One of the most powerful elements of Christian belief is the juxtaposition of strength and weakness. Nowhere is this more evident than in the great anticipation of Advent, the month before Christmas. Nowhere is the Christian liturgy more hopeful—or even, in some ways, more glorious—than in the songs that prepare the way for the coming of the King.

Yet the King is but an infant—scarcely magnificent or terrifying, the usual means by which people perceive power. Time and again, whether in Scripture or in our everyday lives, power is truly measured not so much in terms of strength as it is in endurance. And such strength as the infant King's is to be found more in his promise of things to come than in the grasp of his little fingers.

Melchior Teschner, cantor and schoolmaster at Fraustadt in Silesia, eventually became Lutheran pastor in the nearby village of Oberpritschen.[6] In his day, he was recognized as a fine tunesmith, and some of his work was even published in Leipzig. This tune is perhaps his best-known contribution to the hymnal. It also serves as the melody to "All Glory, Laud, and Honor" (No. 11 in this collection).

---

[6] See *Harvard*, pg. 302.

No. 8: BEHOLD THE KING

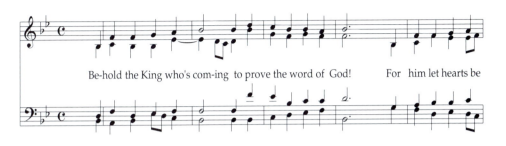

Be-hold the King who's com-ing to prove the word of God! For him let hearts be

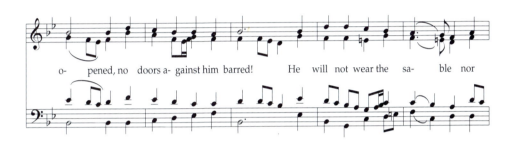

o- pened, no doors a- gainst him barred! He will not wear the sa- ble nor

will he rule on earth; on- ly will the ho- ly per- ceive the king at birth.

Behold the King who's coming to serve the word of God!
His light will be the light of truth to spare us from the dark
Piteous in the shadow we see the slaves of gold
And only those with faith in God will hear the promise told.

Behold the King who's coming to be the word of God!
The word is truth, the word is light, the word is surely love
How vain the search for sceptre, for crown of gold or throne
The word it is the act of God, believe the word alone.

No. 9: Lo! He Comes

Music: St. Thomas, att. **John Francis Wade** (1711-1786)
Words: **Charles Wesley** (1707-1788)

John Francis Wade was an Englishman who spent the greater part of his adult life as a Catholic refugee in France. In the town of Douay, he earned his living copying, selling, and composing church music. Among the best known of his attributed compositions is the Christmas carol "Adeste fideles" ("Come, all ye faithful").

But in that strange way that seems so common in the Episcopal hymnal, the music of a Catholic was coupled by later editors with a text written by a Methodist. Charles Wesley is believed to have composed over six thousand hymns, and it was the strength and surety of his lyrical skill that provided the Methodist church with its foundation during its early years.

The text for "Lo! He Comes" first appeared in Wesley's collection, *Hymns of Intercession for All Mankind*, published in 1758. It has been set on several other occasions, most notably to melodies by Thomas Olivers, another Methodist preacher, and Martin Madan, who adapted Olivers' setting for *Collections of Psalm-Tunes*, published in London in 1769.[7]

---

[7] See *Harvard*, pg. 308.

No. 9: Lo! He Comes

Lo! he comes with clouds descending, once for our salvation slain;
thousand thousand saints attending swell the triumph of his train:
Alleluia! Alleluia! Christ the Lord returns to reign.

Those dear tokens of his passion still his dazzling body bears,
Cause of endless exultation
To his ransomed worshipers;
With what rapture, with what rapture gaze we on those glorious scars!

Yea, amen! let all adore thee, high on thine eternal throne;
Savior, take the power and glory;
Claim the kingdom for thine own:
Alleluia! Alleluia! Thou shalt reign, and thou alone.

No. 10: Sleepers, Awake!

Music: **Hans Sachs** (1494-1576); arr. and harm. **Johann Sebastian Bach** (1685-1750)
Words: **Philipp Nicolai** (1556-1608); trans. **Catherine Winkworth** (1829-78)

Perhaps the most celebrated hymn from Advent is "Sleepers, Awake!" one of the few hymns that has a distinct musical life of its own, thanks primarily to the arrangement and harmonization done by Bach in 1731 for Cantata 140. Hans Sachs, a *Meistersinger* of Nuremburg, had been a shoemaker before being initiated in the art of the meistersinger by a weaver. By his own account, he wrote 4,725 songs, 1,700 fables and tales in verse, and 208 plays. He is probably best known through his characterization in Richard Wagner's opera, *Die Meistersinger*.

The text was one of two included in the back of a volume of meditations written by Philipp Nicolai, a Lutheran pastor, during an outbreak of the plague in 1597. Catherine Winkworth, an advocate for women's higher education in the nineteenth century, was responsible for introducing many German texts to the English with her series of publications, the *Lyra Germanica*. "Sleepers, Awake!" was included in the second series, published in 1858.

The images and ideas conveyed in this translation are typical of the early Reformation. Certain Reformists viewed themselves as the new chosen people and looked upon their own lands as the promised Israel. The idea of being alert, of preparing, of being ready for the coming of the Lord is essential to understanding the fervor with which they preached and practiced their faith in the seventeenth and eighteenth centuries.[8]

[8] See *Harvard*, pg. 288 and pg. 301.

"Wake, a-wake, the night is fly— ing!" the watch-men on the heights are cry- ing. "A-

wake, Je- ru- sa- lem, a- rise!" Mid- night's peace their cry has bro- ken, their ur-gent sum-mons

clear-ly spo- ken: "The time has come, O maid-ens wise! Rise up and give us

light; the Bride-groom is in sight. Al- le- lu- ia! Your lamps pre-pare and

has- ten there, that you may in the wed- ding share.

Zion hears the watchmen singing; her heart with joyful hope is springing
She wakes and hurries through the night.
Forth he comes, her Bridegroom glorious, in strength of grace, in truth victorious:
Her star is risen, her light grows bright.
Now come, most worthy Lord, God's Son, Incarnate Word, Alleluia!
We follow all and heed your call to come into the banquet hall.

Lamb of God, the heavens adore thee; let saints and angels sing before thee,
As harps and cymbals swell the sound.
Twelve great pearls, the city's portals: through them we stream to join the immortals
As we with joy thy throne surround.
No eye has known the sight, no ear heard such delight: Alleluia!
Therefore we sing to greet our King; forever let our praises ring.

No. 11: ALL GLORY, LAUD, AND HONOR

Music: VALET WILL ICH DIR GEBEN, **Melchior Teschner** (1584-1635); harm.
  William Henry Monk (1823-89)
Words: **Theodulph of Orleans** (d. 821); trans. **Rev. John Mason Neale**
  (1818-66)

The celebration of Palm Sunday captures another dynamic conflict of the Christian ideal. Occurring on the Sunday before Passiontide, it marks the triumphant entry of Christ into Jerusalem as the King of the Jews. But just as it was hard to perceive the regal splendor of a child born in a stable, this king is wearing no crown. He has no entourage, and instead of appearing on a fine horse, he is riding a jackass.

Like "Come, Ye Faithful, Raise the Strain" (No. 6), "All Glory, Laud, and Honor" is of mixed lineage. The text, originally in medieval Latin, was translated by a nineteenth-century English cleric; the music is German.

For more on William Henry Monk, please see No. 4, "The Strife Is O'er."

No. 11: ALL GLORY, LAUD, AND HONOR

Refrain

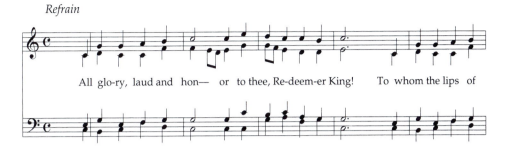

All glo-ry, laud and hon— or to thee, Re-deem-er King! To whom the lips of

Verse

chil- dren made sweet ho-san-nas ring! Thou art the King of Is- ra- el, thou

Da-vid's ro-yal Son, who in the Lord's name com— est, the King and Bless-ed One.

The company of angels is praising thee on high;
and we with all creation in chorus make reply.

The people of the Hebrews with palms before thee went;
our praise and prayers and anthems before thee we present.

(Repeat Refrain)

No. 12: The Joining of the Feast

Music: Land of Rest, traditional American folk melody, arr. **Anthony Newman** (b. 1941)
Words: **Jackson Braider** (b. 1954)

One of the lessons from Martin Luther in matters of hymnody concerns the nature of the tune. If the melody is neither remembered nor memorable, the congregation will have trouble singing it, and if they have trouble singing it, then they will not be joined into a single, powerful voice as they participate in worship. This is one of the reasons why Luther often drew the tunes for his texts from the body of folksong found in his native Thuringia: people already knew the tunes.

It is somewhat strange, then, that the major churches in the United States have been reluctant, until recently, to delve into the great body of American folksong. True, the "folk" mass has had a place in churches since the sixties, but it is generally presented only as an alternative to more standard hymnody and not as a complementary ingredient to the literature.

The tune for Land of Rest represents one of the lesser known elements of European-American lore, the religious song. For many of the European settlers who came to America, this was a land of promise, a land of hope, a land of rest—hence the proliferation of town names like Bethlehem, Bethel, Canaan, Shiloh, and others. Hence, too, the fragmentation of religious practice in this country, as religious communities of many kinds sprang up around the landscape—the Amish, the Shakers, and the Harmonists, to mention a few. The flight from religious persecution in the Old World gave rise to an extraordinary burst of religious freedom and expression in the New.

Land of Rest was originally a song of the world to come, but the beautiful simplicity of the tune lends itself wonderfully to the celebration of the breaking of the bread and the founding of a deeper sense of community among the congregation.

No. 12: The Joining of the Feast

I cry with hun— ger, Lord, you hear me, Lord, you hear my pleas; I know the road — I must fol- low to share the join- ing of the feast.

A promise made, a promise broken
Oaths I swore to thee
I stand amazed; I am forgiven
As you let me join the feast.

Today, this day, in days to come
Lord, I follow thee
My arms around my friends and family
As we join you at the feast.

No. 13: COME WITH US, O BLESSED JESUS

Music: WERDE MUNTER, **Johann Schop** (d. 1667); arr. and harm. **Johann Sebastian Bach** (1685-1750)

Words: **John Henry Hopkins, Jr.** (1820-1891)

Johann Schop was a journeyman musician of the seventeenth century. Originally employed by Duke Friedrich Ulrich at the Hofkapelle at Wolfenbüttel, Schop later joined the court of King Christian IV of Denmark in Copenhagen. In 1621, Schop returned to Germany to serve as the municipal viol player for the city of Hamburg, where he participated in the church music and festivities of the council and the city. Though he was given a great deal of freedom by the Hamburg Council—he visited Copenhagen for an extended period in 1634, where the King attempted to lure him back to service at the court—Schop remained in his post at Hamburg until his death.

As a composer, Schop played an important role in the establishment of the Hamburg school of songwriting. WERDE MUNTER, the tune upon which this hymn is based, is one of many Schop set to sacred texts by Johann Rist. These hymns remain an integral part of the Lutheran repertory.

This particular piece, however, is probably best known for J.S. Bach's arrangement and harmonization. Set to a different text, this hymn is more popularly recognized as "Jesu, Joy of Man's Desiring," a piece that is as well known in the concert hall as it is in the liturgical setting.[9]

[9] For more on Johann Schop, please see entry in *The New Grove's Encyclopedia of Music and Musicians.*

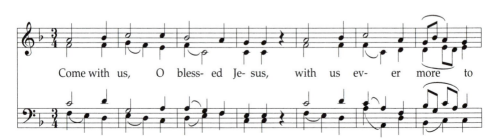

Come with us, O bless- ed Je- sus, with us ev- er more to

see, and though part- ing now thy ta- ble let us nev- er-
more leave thee. Be you now with us for- ev- er, in our
life your love sub- lime our own flesh and blood has ta- ken,
and to us you give your love di- vine.

Come with us, O mighty Savior, God from God, and Light from Light;
You are God, your glory shading, so that we may bear the bright.
Now we go to seek and serve you, through our work as through our prayer;
Grant us light to see and know you, in your people everywhere.

Come with us, O King of glory, by angelic voices be praised;
In our hearts, you in your heaven, let enraptured hymns be raised.
Let the mighty chorus always sing its glad exultant songs;
Let its voice be heard forever, peace for which all mankind longs.

No. 14: Father, We Thank Thee

Music: Rendez à Dieu, att. **Louis Bourgeois** (1510?-1561?)
Words: From the Greek, *c.*110.

Louis Bourgeois is credited with being the musician who contributed the greater part of the Calvinist collection, the *Geneva Psalter*. He derived much of the Psalter from *chanson* (song) melodies, plainchants, and other early settings of psalm translations, often reworking the irregular meter of the original verses of the Biblical translations so that they resembled hymns in form if not in content.[10] Bourgeois also went so far at times as to publish simple polyphonic settings of psalm tunes—*Pseaumes cinquantes de David roy et prophète*, Lyons, 1547—as well as more elaborate settings of wholly original materials. Calvin, who inspired the Puritanical movement throughout the continent as well as in America, did not generally approve of such ornate music.

Rendez à Dieu first appeared in the *Geneva Psalter* in 1551. The text comes from the early church in Greece and was inspired by the Gospel According to St. John (6:25-59). Here, Christ says, "Do not labor for the food which perishes, but for the food which endures to eternal life." It is this portion of the Gospel that inspired the Church in the eighth century to create the sacrament of the Holy Eucharist as it is practiced today.

---

[10] See Howard M. Brown, *Music in the Renaissance*, pg. 276.

No. 14: FATHER, WE THANK THEE

Fa- ther, we thank thee who has plant- ed thy ho- ly Name with-in our minds.

Know-ledge and faith and life im- mor- tal Je- sus thy Son with us will find. You

Lord, did make all for thy plea- sure, did give us food for all our lives,

giv- ing in Christ the Bread e- ter- nal; yours is the pow'r, yours is the praise.

Watch o'er thy Church, O Lord, in mercy,
Save it from evil, guard it still
Perfect it in thy love, unite it,
Cleansed and conformed unto thy will.
As grain, once scattered on the hillsides,
Was in this broken bread made one,
So from all lands thy Church be gathered
Into thy Kingdom by thy Son.

No. 15: LORD, DISMISS US WITH THY BLESSING

Music: SICILIAN MARINERS, Sicilian melody; first published in
The European Magazine and London Review, 1792.
Words: att. **John Fawcett** (1739-1817)

As we have already seen, those responsible for the collection and editing of the many hymnals that began to circulate among British congregations drew their works—both words and music—from a wide and varied group of sources.

Take, for example, this hymn, attributed to one of the ancestors of the celebrated Fawcett family of musicians from the West Riding of Yorkshire. The tune had first appeared in a periodical at the end of the eighteenth century before John Fawcett, a shoemaker and sometime psalmodist, used it as the accompaniment to one of his texts.

There were at least thirty-six professional musicians who descended from this shoemaker, though none rose to any great stature. However, several did make their marks in psalmody and hymnody, most notably Fawcett's grandson and great-grandson, both named John.

Another Fawcett, Joshua, the son of a textile manufacturer, was a cleric who not only wrote on church architecture, but also published in 1845 *Lyra ecclesiastica*, a collection of church music by "eminent living composers." Dedicated to Queen Adelaide, it featured a preface by William Henry Havergal (see No. 28, "God, My King, Thy Might Confessing").[11]

---

[11] See "Fawcett" in *The New Grove's Encyclopedia of Music and Musicians.*

No. 15: Lord, Dismiss Us with Thy Blessing

Lord, dis- miss us with thy bless-ing; fill our hearts with joy and peace;

let us each, thy love pos-sess- ing, tri- umph in re- deem-ing grace;

O, re- fresh us, O, re- fresh us, tra-vel-ing through this wil- der- ness.

Thanks we give and adoration for thy Gospel's joyful sound:
may the fruits of thy salvation in our hearts and lives abound
ever faithful, ever faithful to thy truth may we be found;

so that when thy love shall call us, Savior, from the world away,
fear of death shall not appall us, glad thy summons to obey.
May we ever, may we ever reign with thee in endless day.

No. 16: My God, Thy Table Now Is Spread

Music: ROCKINGHAM, ca. 1780; adapt. **Edward Miller** (1731-1807); harm.
  Samuel Webbe the Elder (1740-1816)
Words: Sts. 1-3, **Philip Doddridge** (1702-51); st. 4, **Isaac Watts** (1674-1748)

Philip Doddridge was Congregational minister at Castle Hill, Northampton for the greater part of his life. During his ministry, he composed over three hundred hymns, and is considered one of the greatest of the English Congregationalist hymn writers.[12] The most prolific Congregationalist hymn writer, however, was Isaac Watts, who composed the fourth verse featured here. His contribution to the literature is an astounding six hundred hymns. It is easy to understand how he is considered by many to be the father of English hymnody.

Indeed, it was Watts who led English Nonconformist churches away from the paraphrase of psalms that characterized congregational singing into the eighteenth century. He worked on behalf of what he called "Spiritual Songs of a more evangelic frame" in assembling his celebrated collection, *Hymns and Spiritual Songs*.

ROCKINGHAM as a tune first appeared in Aaron Williams' *Psalmody in Miniature*, published in 1783. Then Edward Miller, a parish organist in Yorkshire, adapted it for a collection, *Psalms of David for the Use of Parish Churches*, that he published in London in 1790.[13]

Hymn enthusiasts may recognize this as the tune for another Watts text, "When I Survey the Wondrous Cross," a hymn generally sung during the season of Lent.

---

[12] See *Harvard*, pps. 299-300.
[13] *Ibid*, pg. 310.

No. 16: My God, Thy Table Now Is Spread

My God, thy ta- ble now is spread, thy cup with love doth o- ver- flow; be all thy chil- dren thith- er led, and let them thy sweet mer- cies know.

O, let thy table honored be,
and furnished well with joyful guests;
and may each soul salvation see,
this here its sacred pledges taste.

Drawn by thy quickening grace, O Lord,
in countless numbers let them come
and gather from their Father's board
the Bread that lives beyond the tomb.

No. 17: Crown Him with Many Crowns

Music: Diademata, **George Job Elvey** (1816-1893)
Words: **Matthew Bridges** (1800-1894)

Anglicanism—that is, the Church of England—has had a long and, some might say, strange history. Started by Henry VIII in the sixteenth century when he broke with Rome, the Anglican Church of all the Northern European traditions has continued to have the closest affinity with the Roman Catholic faith. Indeed, whenever the Anglican Church has undergone spiritual division, as it did in the course of the Oxford Movement in the first half of the nineteenth century, separatists have tended to turn their allegiance to Rome.

Matthew Bridges was a product of the Oxford Movement. A convert to Catholicism in 1848, he composed a number of hymn collections, most notably *Hymns of the Heart*. "Crown Him with Many Crowns" appeared in the second edition, published in 1851.

George Job Elvey was organist for almost half a century at St. George's Chapel, Windsor Castle, and contributed to many of the hymnals that were assembled and collected in the course of the nineteenth century, most notably E. H. Thorne's *Selection of Psalm and Hymn Tunes* (London, 1858) and *Hymns Ancient and Modern*, perhaps the most influential hymnbook published at the time.

Elvey composed this tune specifically for Bridges' text and included it as part of the Appendix of the 1868 edition of *Hymns Ancient and Modern*.

No. 17: Crown Him with Many Crowns

Crown him with ma- ny crowns, the Lamb up- on his throne; Hark! how the heaven- ly an- them drowns all mu- sic but its own; a- wake, my soul and sing of him who died for thee, and hail him as the match- less King through all e- ter- ni- ty.

Crown him the Son of God before the worlds began,
and ye, who tread where he hath trod,
crown him the Son of man;
who every grief hath known that wrings the human breast,
and takes and bears them for his own,
that all in him may rest.

Crown him the Lord of life, who triumphed o'er the grave,
and rose victorious in the strife
for those he came to save;
his glories now we sing, who died, and rose on high,
who died, eternal life to bring,
and lives that death may die.

No. 18: Lift Up Your Heads
originally *Macht Hoch die Tür*

Music: Truro, melody from *Psalmodia Evangelica, Part II*, 1789; harm.
    Lowell Mason (1792-1872)
Words: **Georg Weissel** (1590-1635); trans. **Catherine Winkworth** (1827-78)

This is another of the German hymns introduced to English-speaking congregations by Catherine Winkworth in her collections *Lyra Germanica* (1855 and 1858) and *The Chorale Book for England* (1863).[14]

Georg Weissel, a Lutheran pastor in Königsberg, was a member of the Poetical Union there, and had drawn the inspiration for this work from Psalm 24 ("The earth is the Lord's, and all that therein is..."). First published in *Preussische Fest-Lieder* (Part I, published in Elbing, 1642), the hymn had originally been intended for the first Sunday in Advent.

But in the translation from Lutheran to Anglican usage, the hymn was not only displaced from Advent, it experienced a change of accompaniment. The tune as it appeared in J.A. Freylinghausen's *Geistreiches Gesang-Buch* (1704) was replaced by an English melody, Truro, which had been taken from a late eighteenth-century collection of religious melodies.

---

[14] See *Harvard*, pps. 288-89 and pg. 302.

No. 18: Lift Up Your Heads

Lift up your heads, ye might-y gates; be-hold the King of glo-ry waits! The King of kings is draw-ing near, the Sa-vior of the world is here.

O blest the land, the city blest,
where Christ the ruler is confessed!
O happy hearts and happy homes
to whom this King of triumph comes!

Fling wide the portals of your heart;
make it a temple, set apart
from earthly use for heaven's employ,
adorned with prayer and love and joy.

No. 19: Alleluia! Sing to Jesus!

Music: Hyfrydol, **Rowland Hugh Prichard** (1811-1887)
Words: **William Chatterton Dix** (1837-1898)

William Chatterton Dix was the manager of a marine insurance company in Glasgow, Scotland as well as the author of numerous volumes of hymns. His work had been included in *Hymns Ancient and Modern*, perhaps the most influential and popular English hymnbook of the nineteenth century.

For his part, Rowland Hugh Prichard was a Welshman, a precentor (music leader) in Cardiff. Interestingly, he left the church in later life and became a loom tender's assistant in a flannel mill. Hyfrydol, written by Prichard when he wasn't even twenty years old, counts among the most popular tunes in hymnody, being used to accompany no less than four different texts in various Protestant collections, including the one used here. Some may recognize this as the tune for "Praise the Lord, ye heavens, adore him," Charles Wesley's "Love divine, all loves excelling," and William Cowper's "Hear, what God, the Lord, hath spoken."[15]

[15] See *Harvard*, pg. 290 and pg. 304.

his the throne; Al- le- lu- ia! his the tri- umph

his the vic- to- ry a- lone; Hark! the songs of peace- ful

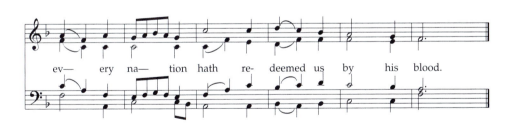

Zi- on thun- der like a might- y flood; Je- sus out of

ev— ery na— tion hath re- deemed us by his blood.

Alleluia! Bread of Heaven,
thou on earth our food, our stay!
Alleluia! here the sinful
flee to thee from day to day:
Intercessor, friend of sinners,
Earth's Redeemer, plead for me,
where the songs of all the sinless
sweep across the crystal sea.

Alleluia! King eternal,
thee the Lord of lords we own:
Alleluia! born of Mary, earth thy footstool
heaven thy throne:
thou within the veil hast entered,
robed in flesh, our great High Priest:
thou on earth both Priest and Victim
in the eucharistic feast.

No. 20: Holy God, We Praise Thy Name

Music: Grosser Gott, melody from *Katholisches Gesangbuch*, 1686; after
   Conrad Kocher (1786-1832); harm. **Anthony Newman** (b. 1941)
Words: Paraphrase of *Te Deum*; sts. 1-4, **Ignaz Franz** (1719-1790), trans.
   Clarence Walworth (1820-1900)

The Anglicans of England were not the only people looking to different religious traditions for materials to inspire their congregations. Conrad Kocher, organist of the Stiftskirche in Stuttgart, drew this melody from the *Katholisches Gesangbuch*, a Catholic collection assembled during the Counter-Reformation. Kocher himself was recognized as one of the leading figures in the revitalization of German church music in the early nineteenth century, largely because of his investigations of older religious collections.

The text is the translation of a paraphrase of the *Te Deum*, an ancient hymn of the Western Church ("We praise Thee, O God, we acknowledge Thee to be the Lord..."). Ascribed in legend to an ecstatic outburst on the part of St. Ambrose upon the baptism of St. Augustine, it is now reckoned to be the work of Bishop Nicetas of Dacia (*c.*335-414). Often sung at Morning Prayer in the Anglican and Episcopalian traditions, the *Te Deum* is the chief hymn of rejoicing in the Catholic church.

No. 20: Holy God, We Praise Thy Name

Ho- ly God, we praise thy Name, Lord of all, we
bow be- fore thee; all on earth thy scep- ter claim,
all in heaven a- bove a- dore thee; in— fi- nite thy
vast do- main, ev— er- last- ing is thy reign.

Hark, the loud celestial hymn angel choirs above are raising;
cherubim and seraphim, in unceasing chorus praising,
fill the heavens with sweet accord:
holy, holy, holy Lord!

Holy Father, Holy Son, Holy Spirit, Three we name thee,
while in essence only One, undivided God we claim thee;
then, adoring, bend the knee
and confess the mystery.

No. 21: Come, Thou Almighty King

Music: Moscow (also known as Trinity), **Felice de Giardini** (1716-1796); harm. based on *Hymns Ancient and Modern*, 1875, and **Lowell Mason** (1792-1872)
Words: Anon., ca. 1757

"Come, Thou Almighty King" is a fine example of how far and to what extent the editors and compilers of the *Hymns Ancient and Modern* series went in assembling their materials. As we saw with "Lord, Dismiss Us with Thy Blessing" (No. 15 in this volume), they tended to combine lyrics and melodies with little regard as to the compatability of sources. In this case, they took a tune with a Slavic title written by an Italian residing in London and used it as an accompaniment to an anonymous lyric that had been inserted as an afterthought into an eighteenth-century English hymnbook.

Felice de Giardini was an Italian violinist who served as Concertmaster of the orchestra of the Italian Opera in London before returning to Italy to serve in the household of the Ambassador to Sardinia. The tune was published in the *Collection of Psalm and Hymn Tunes* (1769) by Martin Madan, chaplain of the Lock Hospital and made its first appearance with this text at that time, though it later came to be used as the accompaniment to "Thou, Whose Almighty Word," written by John Marriott in 1813.

"Come, Thou Almighty King" first appeared in print as part of a four-page tract bound with copies of the 1757 edition of George Whitefield's *Collection of Hymns*.[16]

[16]See *Harvard*, pg. 325.

No. 21: Come, Thou Almighty King

Come, thou al-might-y King, help us thy
Name to sing, help us to praise.
Fa-ther whose love un-known all things cre-at-ed own,
build in our hearts thy throne, An-cient of Days.

Come, thou incarnate Word, by heaven and earth adored;
our prayer attend:
come, and thy people bless; come, give thy word success;
'Stablish thy righteousness, Savior and friend.

To Thee, great One in Three, the highest praises be,
hence evermore;
thy sovereign majesty may we in glory see,
and to eternity love and adore.

No. 22: HOLY, HOLY, HOLY!

Music: NICAEA, **John Bacchus Dykes** (1823-76)
Words: **Reginald Heber** (1783-1826)

Reginald Heber played a significant role in the effort to introduce hymn-singing into the Anglican Church. Into the nineteenth century, the congregation generally sang traditional paraphrases of the psalms. While vicar of Hodnet in Shropshire, Heber began work on a collection of hymns for the Church Year, drawing examples not only from previous hymnody, but soliciting texts from contemporary poets and contributing a few of his own as well.

Heber's appointment as Bishop of Calcutta in 1823 and his untimely death stopped him from seeing the collection reach print. But when his widow published *Hymns written and adapted to the weekly church service of the year* in 1827, this hymnal became so popular that it went into a second edition the following year before being taken up by the Episcopal Church in the United States. The effect was to establish the place of the hymn in the Anglican tradition.

It was not until 1861, however, that "Holy, Holy, Holy!" first appeared with this setting. John Bacchus Dykes, a minor canon and precentor at Durham Cathedral, set NICAEA to Heber's text in the first edition of *Hymns Ancient and Modern*. Dykes during his lifetime composed over three hundred different hymn tunes and did more than perhaps any other composer in forming the style of Anglican church music as we know it today.[17]

---

[17] See *Harvard*, pps. 324-5.

No. 22: HOLY, HOLY, HOLY!

Ho- ly, ho- ly, ho- ly! Lord God Al- might- y!

Ear- ly in the morn- ing our song shall rise to thee:

Ho- ly, ho- ly, ho- ly! mer- ci- ful and might- y,

God in three Per- sons, bless- ed Tri- ni- ty.

Holy, Holy, Holy! all the saints adore thee,
casting down their golden crowns around the glassy sea;
cherubim and seraphim falling down before thee,
which wert, and art, and evermore shalt be.

Holy, Holy, Holy! Lord God Almighty!
All thy works shall praise thy Name, in earth and sky and sea;
Holy, Holy, Holy! merciful and mighty,
God in three Persons, blessed Trinity.

No. 23: ROCK OF AGES

Music: TOPLADY, **Thomas Hastings** (1784-1872)
Words: **Augustus Montague Toplady** (1740-78)

Born in Washington, Connecticut, Thomas Hastings was the albino son of a country doctor. When the family moved to central New York State at the very end of the eighteenth century, Hastings turned to music, becoming the leader of a church choir by the time he was eighteen. Over his lifetime, he compiled a number of books of hymns, including *Musica Sacra* (1816) and *Spiritual Songs* (with Lowell Mason, 1831).

Augustus Montague Toplady was by all accounts a stormy character in spite of his constant devotion to the service of God. Born in England and educated in Ireland, he was first enthralled by John Wesley's Methodism. A bitter dispute with Wesley, resulting from Toplady's apparently extreme views, led the cleric to seek ordination in the Church of England in 1762. Even here, however, he was not content. By 1775, he abandoned the Church of England in favor of the more astringent beliefs of the Calvinists, with whom he served as a preacher as late as 1775.

Best known for his prose work, Toplady published three sets of writings toward the end of his life: *Historic Proof of the Doctrinal Calvinism of the Church of England* (1774) and *Poems on Sacred Subjects wherein The Fundamental Doctrines of Christianity, with many other interesting Points ...* (1769), and his *Psalms and Hymns for Public and Private Worship* (1776).

"Rock of Ages" has been in hymnals since 1826, and is probably the best known composition of both Hastings and Toplady.[18]

---

[18] See *The Hymnal 1940 Companion*, pgs. 292, 454-455, and 577-578.

No. 23: Rock of Ages

Rock of A- ges cleft for me, let me hide my-self in thee; let the

wa- ter and the blood from thy wound- ed side that flowed, be of

sin the dou-ble cure, cleanse me from its guilt and power.

Should my tears forever flow,
should my zeal no languor know,
all for sin could not atone:
thou must save, and thou alone;
in my hand no price I bring,
simply to thy cross I cling.

While I draw this fleeting breath,
when mine eyelids close in death,
when I rise to worlds unknown
and behold thee on thy throne,
Rock of ages, cleft for me,
let me hide myself in thee.

No. 24: O God, Our Help in Ages Past

Music: St. Anne, att. **William Croft** (1678-1727); harm. **William Henry Monk** (1823-1889)
Words: **Isaac Watts** (1674-1748)

Isaac Watts is unparalleled in the scope of his contribution to English hymnody—over six hundred songs, with some two dozen still appearing in a variety of hymn books from all faiths. This text, an exquisite paraphrase of Psalm 90, verses 1-5 ("Lord, thou hast been our refuge: from one generation to another..."), was first published in his *Psalms of David Imitated in the Language of the New Testament, And apply'd to the Christian State and Worship* (London, 1719).

The tune, St. Anne, appeared anonymously in the *Supplement to the New Version of Psalms* (6th ed., 1708), where it accompanied yet another paraphrase of a psalm, this one of Psalm 42 ("Like as the hart desireth the waterbrooks: so longeth my soul after thee, O God..."). William Croft, to whom this tune has been traditionally attributed, was organist and composer to the Chapel Royal and also served as organist at Westminster Abbey.

Bach enthusiasts will immediately recognize the tune as the first theme of the spectacular triple fugue in E-flat major with which he closes his *Lutheran Organ Mass*.

No. 24: O God, Our Help in Ages Past

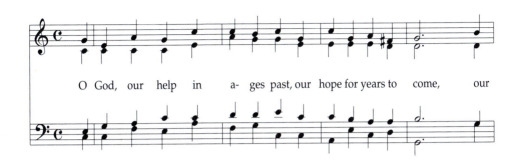

O God, our help in a- ges past, our hope for years to come, our

shel- ter from the storm- y blast and our e- ter- nal home:

Under the shadow of thy throne thy saints have dwelt secure;
sufficient is thine arm alone, and our defense is sure.

Before the hills in order stood, or earth received her frame,
for everlasting thou art God, to endless years the same.

A thousand ages in thy sight are like an evening gone;
short as the watch that ends the night before the rising sun.

Time, like an ever-rolling stream, bears all our years away;
they fly, forgotten, as a dream dies at the opening day.

O God, our help in ages past, our hope for years to come,
be thou our guide while life shall last, and our eternal home.

No. 25: Amazing Grace

Music: New Britain, from *Virginia Harmony*, 1831; adapt. att. **Edwin Othello Excell** (1851-1921)
Words: **John Newton** (1725-1807)

"Amazing Grace" was first published, with the assistance of William Cowper, in the influential collection, *Olney Hymns*, in 1779.

The story of its author John Newton is essentially the story told in this hymn. After leading the dissolute life of a seaman in the Royal Navy, John Newton underwent conversion after reading Thomas à Kempis' *Imitation of Christ*. Returning to Liverpool, he became a surveyor of the tides while he studied for the clergy, and was ordained as the curate of Olney, Buckinghamshire, in 1753. In 1779, he became rector of St. Mary Woolnoth in London, where he worked until his death in 1807.

The music as we know it today comes from one of the many regional collections of songs and tunes that were published throughout the United States in the first half of the nineteenth century.

Today, it is impossible to separate the tune from the lyric, and "Amazing Grace" counts among the most recorded and performed songs of all time, cutting across stylistic lines from African American gospel to folk and jazz, as well as classical music.

No. 25: Amazing Grace

A- maz- ing grace! how sweet the sound, that

saved a wretch like me! I once was lost but

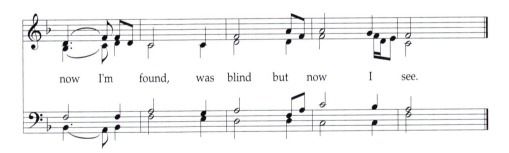

now I'm found, was blind but now I see.

'Twas grace that taught my heart to fear,
and grace my fears relieved;
how precious did that grace appear
the hour I first believed!

The Lord has promised good to me,
his word my hope secures;
he will my shield and portion be
as long as life endures.

When we've been there ten thousand years,
bright shining as the sun,
we've no less days to sing our praise
than when we'd first begun.

No. 26: Abide with Me

Music: Eventide, **William Henry Monk** (1823-1889)
Words: **Henry Francis Lyte** (1793-1847)

Henry Francis Lyte was curate of Lower Brixham, Devon, from 1823 until his death, and derived much of his work from paraphrases of the psalms—most notably, "God of mercy, God of grace," a paraphrase of Psalm 67 and "Praise my soul, the King of heaven," a paraphrase of Psalm 103, both contained in Lyte's collection *Spirit of the Psalms* (1834).

"Abide with Me," Lyte's most famous lyric, is not a psalm paraphrase, though the theme of calling upon the Lord is pervasive in the Psalter. Written in the last year of Lyte's life (1847), the text was set to music by William Henry Monk (please see Nos. 4 and 11). Monk, the first music editor of the collection *Hymns Ancient and Modern* (1861), included "Abide with Me" in the first edition of that celebrated collection.

No. 26: Abide with Me

A- bide with me: fast falls the e- ven- tide;

the dark-ness deep- ens; Lord, with me a- bide:

when o- ther help- ers fail and com-forts flee,

help of the help- less, O a- bide with me.

I need thy presence every passing hour;
what but thy grace can foil the tempter's power?
Who, like thyself, my guide and stay can be?
Through cloud and sunshine, Lord, abide with me.

I fear no foe, with thee at hand to bless;
ills have no weight, and tears no bitterness.
Where is death's sting? where, grave, thy victory?
I triumph still, if thou abide with me.

No. 27: Joyful, Joyful, We Adore Thee

Music: Hymn to Joy, **Ludwig van Beethoven** (1770-1827); adapt.
    Edward Hodges (1796-1867)
Words: **Henry Van Dyke** (1852-1933)

    Henry Van Dyke was, among other things, a Presbyterian minister, an educator, a statesman, and a writer. At one time the pastor of the Brick Presbyterian Church in New York City, he later went on to teach English literature at Princeton, serve as the U.S. minister to the Netherlands, and hold the post of Navy chaplain. He wrote a number of inspirational texts, including *The Other Wise Man* (1896), as well as various collections of poems and essays. Another hymn by Van Dyke, "Jesus, thou divine Companion," was included in the Episcopal hymnal of 1940.

    Ludwig van Beethoven was a Catholic, and it might very well be that his upbringing outside Protestant circles did not lead him to pursue hymn writing—with its chorale setting—more actively in the course of his work. The Hymn to Joy used here was extracted from the fourth movement of his Ninth Symphony, in which he used both choir and soloists as well as a full orchestra.

    Though Beethoven wrote several masses and cantatas, his contributions to the modern hymn books are comprised solely of melodies taken from larger works.

No. 27: Joyful, Joyful, We Adore Thee

Joy- ful, joy- ful, we a- dore thee, God of glo- ry, Lord of love;

hearts un- fold like flowers be- fore thee, prais- ing thee, their sun a- bove.

Melt the clouds of sin and sad- ness; drive the dark of doubt a- way; giv-

er of im- mor- tal glad- ness, fill us with the light of day.

All thy works with joy surround thee, earth and heaven reflect thy rays,
stars and angels sing around thee, center of unbroken praise.
Field and forest, vale and mountain, blooming meadow, flashing sea,
chanting bird and flowing fountain, call us to rejoice in thee.

Thou art giving and forgiving, ever blessing, ever blest,
wellspring of the joy of living, oceandepth of happy rest!
Thou our Father, Christ our Brother: all who live in love are thine;
teach us how to love each other, lift us to the joy divine.

No. 28: God, My King, Thy Might Confessing

Music: STUTTGART, att. **Christian Friedrich Witt** (1660-1716), melody
 from *Psalmodia Sacra, oder Andächtige und Schöne Gesänge*, 1715;
 adapt. and harm. **William Henry Havergal** (1793-1870)
Words: **Richard Mant** (1776-1848)

The tune upon which this hymn is based, STUTTGART, was probably written by Christian Friedrich Witt, Kapellmeister to the Prince of Gotha and Altenburg. The collection from which it was taken, *Psalmodia Sacra*, was edited by Witt for use in the principality of Gotha and Altenburg. Since the tune was published as part of *Hymns Ancient and Modern*, it has been used with a number of different texts, from Charles Wesley's "Come, thou long-expected Jesus" to James Montgomery's paraphrase of Psalm 91, "Call Jehovah thy Salvation."

William Henry Havergal, a native of Buckinghamshire, turned to musical pursuits during a lengthy convalescence following a carriage accident. Weakened by his ordeal, he nevertheless became a champion of musical reform in the Church of England and edited several important studies and collections of hymns.

Richard Mant, who composed the text, was a bishop in the Church of Ireland who did a great deal of writing in both verse and prose. He even versified portions of his sermons and published a volume of poetic sketches called *The Gospel Miracles*. He introduced much of the Roman Breviary to the English reader and translated both psalms and Latin sources.

Mant is believed to have provided much influence to Reginald Heber in the preparation of *Hymns written and adapted to the weekly church service of the year* (please see No. 22, "Holy, Holy, Holy!" for more information on Heber).[19]

---

[19] Harvey Blair Marks, *The rise and growth of English hymnody*, pps. 122-123.

No. 28: God, My King, Thy Might Confessing

God, my King, thy might con-fess-ing, ev- er will I bless thy Name;

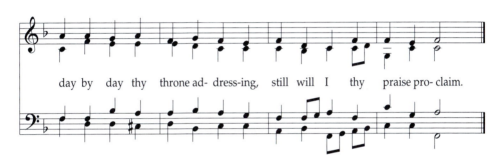

day by day thy throne ad- dress-ing, still will I thy praise pro- claim.

Honor great our God befitteth; who his majesty can reach?
Age to age his works transmitteth, age to age his power shall teach.

They shall talk of all thy glory, on thy might and greatness dwell,
speak of thy dread acts the story, and thy deeds of wonder tell.

Nor shall fail from memory's treasure works by love and mercy wrought,
works of love surpassing measure, works of mercy passing thought.

Full of kindness and compassion, slow to anger, vast in love,
God is good to all creation; all his works his goodness prove.

All thy works, O Lord, shall bless thee; thee shall all thy saints adore:
King supreme shall they confess thee, and proclaim thy sovereign power.

No. 29: Fairest Lord Jesus, Ruler of All Nature

Music: St. Elizabeth, melody from *Schlesische Volkslieder*, 1842; arr.
Anthony Newman (b. 1941)
Words: German composite, dated 1677, trans. pub. New York, 1850

Perhaps the single most influential movement at the turn of the nineteenth century was that of the Romantic Nationalists. Fostered by the likes of Wilhelm and Jakob Grimm in Germany, and William Wordsworth and William Blake in England, it was primarily a response to the effects of the Industrial Revolution and the displacement of millions of rural inhabitants in order to run the factories. Recognizing the potential loss of hundreds of years of culture, the Grimms and others devoted much of their lives to collecting the stories, customs, and music of local peoples. Some of these collections, like those of the Brothers Grimm, have become permanent features of the modern imagination.

Schlesische Volkslieder was a collection of folksongs gathered in the northwest of Germany in the first half of the nineteenth century. The folk-like nature of St. Elizabeth is reinforced here by the choice of text used to accompany it; "Fairest Lord Jesus," a composite of different German texts from the seventeenth century, is almost as much a eulogy of the natural world as it is of Christ.

In its celebration of the nature, "Fairest Lord Jesus" resembles William Blake's "A New Jerusalem" (1804), but it stops short of the Englishman's social criticism. While the German hymn simply glorifies nature, Blake sets nature in opposition to man's own creation, "the dark satanic mills" of the Industrial Revolution.

No. 29: Fairest Lord Jesus, Ruler of All Nature

Fair- est Lord Je- sus, Ru- ler of all na- ture, O thou of God and man the Son; thee will I cher- ish, thee will I hon- or, thou, my soul's glo-r-y, joy and crown.

Fair are the meadows, fairer still the woodlands,
robed in the blooming garb of spring:
Jesus is fairer, Jesus is purer,
who makes the woeful heart to sing.

Fair is the sunshine, fairer still the moonlight,
and all the twinkling, starry host:
Jesus shines brighter, Jesus shines purer,
than all the angels heaven can boast.

No. 30: Now Thank We All Our God

Music: Nun danket alle Gott, melody **Johann Cruger** (1598-1662);
harm. **William Henry Monk** (1823-89), after **Felix
Mendelssohn-Bartholdy** (1809-47)
Words: **Martin Rinckart** (1586-1649); trans. **Catherine Winkworth** (1827-78)

Martin Rinckart was a Lutheran pastor in Eilenburg,
Saxony during the time of the Thirty Years' War (1618-1648),
which pitted France, Sweden, Denmark, and England against the
Holy Roman Empire, based in Austria. Most of the fighting took
place in Germany, bringing plague and famine to many regions
of the land.

This hymn was probably first published in a collection of
Rinckart's work, *Jesu Herz-Büchlein* (1636), though it may have
been written as early as 1630 to mark the centennary of Martin
Luther's Augsburg Confession. Catherine Winkworth (see No.
10, "Sleepers, Awake!") first brought the lyric to the attention of
English-speaking congregations in *Lyra Germanica*.[20]

Johann Crüger was cantor of the Lutheran Cathedral of St.
Nicholas in Berlin and the composer of many chorale melodies.
Crüger was responsible for creating *Praxis pietatis melica* (Berlin,
1647), one of the finest examples of German hymnals from the
seventeenth century. By 1736, the work had gone through no less
than forty-four different editions. Crüger was greatly influenced
by the *Geneva Psalter*, first prepared by Louis Bourgeois (see No.
14).

Felix Mendelssohn was born to a prominent Jewish family
in Berlin—his aunt Sarah had been a patron of Bach's eldest son,
Wilhelm Friedemann. Mendelssohn himself was a convert to
Lutheranism and was responsible for instigating the great Bach
revival of the nineteenth century with a performance of the *St.
Matthew Passion* in 1827. Nun danket alle Gott was one of numerous chorales harmonized by Mendelssohn in what he considered to be the "old style" of hymn writing.

[20] See *Harvard*, pps. 288-9 and pps. 290-1.

No. 30: Now Thank We All Our God

Now thank we all our God, with heart and hands and voi- ces, who won-drous things hath done, in whom his world re- joi- ces; who from our mo- ther's arms hath blessed us on our way with count-less gifts of love, and still is ours to- day.

O may this bounteous God through all our lives be near us!
with everjoyful hearts and blessed peace to cheer us;
and keep us in his grace, and guide us when perplexed,
and free us from all ills in this world and the next.

All praise and thanks to God the Father now be given,
the Son, and him who reigns with them in highest heaven,
eternal, Triune God, whom earth and heaven adore;
for thus it was, is now, and shall be, evermore.

No. 31: God the Omnipotent

Music: Russia, **Alexis Lvov** (1799-1870)
Words: Sts. 1-2, **Henry Fothergill Chorley** (1808-1872); sts. 3-4, **John Ellerton** (1826-1893)

Of all the hymns contained in this small volume, "God the Omnipotent," probably has the most fractured history. As with so many of the hymns included here, this is one of mixed parentage; a Russian government official, a music critic for the *Times* of London, and an English clergyman unite very different inspirations in this singular piece.

The first two verses, by Henry Fothergill Chorley (the music critic) were originally part of a hymn called "In Time of War." The second pair of verses was penned at the height of the Franco-Prussian War in 1870 by the Reverend John Ellerton, who followed Chorley's inspiration.

The tune was composed by Alexis Lvov in response to Tsar Nicholas I's command for a new national anthem. Pleased with his labor, the Tsar made Lvov director of music in the Imperial Chapel.[21] When Chorley used the tune to accompany his text, the melody was dubbed "Russia" or "The Russian Hymn."

Russia is also used as the accompaniment for "Christ the Victorious," a hymn typically used in connection with the burial service.

---

[21]See *Harvard*, pg. 342.

No. 31: God the Omnipotent

God the Om- ni- po-tent! King, who or- dain- est
thun- der thy clar- ion, the light- ning thy sword;
show forth thy pi- ty on high where thou reign- est:
give to us peace in our time, O Lord.

God the Allmerciful! earth hath forsaken
thy ways all holy, and slighted thy word;
bid not thy wrath in its terrors awaken:
give to us peace in our time, O Lord.

God the Allprovident! earth by thy chastening
yet shall to freedom and truth be restored;
through the thick darkness thy kingdom is hastening:
thou wilt give peace in thy time, O Lord.

God the Allrighteous One! earth hath defied thee;
yet to eternity standeth thy word,
falsehood and wrong shall not tarry beside thee:
give to us peace in our time, O Lord.

No. 32: Coventry Carol

Music: Coventry Carol, melody from *Pageant of the Shearmen and Tailors*
(15th cent.), arr. **Anthony Newman** (b. 1941)
Words: Coventry carol, 15th cent.

Little of early English hymnody—that is, spiritual versification predating the eighteenth century—remains; however, a number of carols and related works of religious instruction have survived, among them this carol from the *Pageant of the Shearmen and Tailors*, which dates from the 1400s.

Carols are generally distinguished from hymns in the Middle Ages by the absence of learned languages—Latin, for example, or Greek. Indeed, they were the only examples of vernacular religious writing prior to the Reformation. Sponsored by local guilds for holidays and festivals, these pageants contributed to the foundation of European drama, conveying a religious subject through a simple narrative, acted out generally by guild members as a means of raising money for anything from a charity to the building of a cathedral.

Pageants, like the medieval Mystery plays, contained both verse and music. Much of the music has been lost. Fortunately, both the text and the tune of the "Coventry Carol" survived.[22]

---

[22]Adam Fox, *English Hymns and Hymn Writers*, pps. 10-12.

No. 32: COVENTRY CAROL

Herod the King, in his raging charged
he hath this day his men of might,
in his own sight,
all young children to slay.

That woe is me, poor child for thee!
And every morn and day, for thy parting
nor say nor sing
bye-bye, lully, lullay.

(Repeat Burden)

No. 33: The Duteous Day Now Closeth

Music: O WELT, ICH MUSS DICH LASSEN, melody att. **Heinrich Isaac** (1450?-1517); harm. **Johann Sebastian Bach** (1685-1750)
Words: **Paulus Gerhardt** (1607-1676); trans. **Robert Seymour Bridges** (1844-1930)

This hymn has had a long and illustrious history, beginning in the court of Emperor Maximilian I, to whom Heinrich Isaac (also spelled "Isaak") was composer. It first appeared in print in Georg Förster's *Ein Ausszug guter alter Teutscher liedlein* (Nürnberg, 1539), where it accompanied a text entitled "Innsbruck, ich muss dich lassen" (Innsbruck, I must leave you). The tune's first appearance with this text—Oh World, I must leave you—was in the 1647 edition of Johann Crüger's *Praxis pietatis melica*.[23]

To many music enthusiasts, however, this tune is probably best remembered for its on-going use in Johann Sebastian Bach's *St. Matthew Passion*, where it serves as one of the chorales that unify the work as a whole. It is Bach's harmonization that is used here.

[23] See *Harvard*, pg. 299.

No. 33: The Duteous Day Now Closeth

The du-teous day now clos- eth, each flower and tree re- pos- eth, shade creeps o'er wild and wood: let us, as night is fall- ing, on God our Ma- ker call- ing, give thanks to him, the Gi- ver good.

Now all the heavenly splendor
breaks forth in starlight and worlds unknown;
and we, this marvel seeing, forget our selfish being
for joy of beauty not our own.

Though long our mortal blindness
has missed God's loving kindness and plunged us into strife;
yet when life's day is over, shall death's fair night discover
the fields of everlasting life.

No. 34: GLORIOUS THINGS OF THEE ARE SPOKEN

Music: AUSTRIA, **Franz Josef Haydn** (1732-1809)
Words: **John Newton** (1725-1807)

This is another hymn whose tune was originally composed as a national anthem. This time, Franz Josef Haydn was writing at the suggestion of the Imperial Chancellor who was looking for an Austrian equivalent of "God Save our Gracious King" (see No. 38, "My Country 'Tis of Thee," below). Interestingly enough, Haydn drew his inspiration for the melody from a Croatian folksong. Set to the text "Gott erhalte Franz den Kaiser" by the Court Poet Lorenz Hauschka, the tune was first sung on the birthday of Emperor Francis II on February 12, 1797.

The tune was subsequently used in various quarters—not all of which would have met Haydn's approval. Haydn himself used the melody in theme and variations in the slow movement of his String Quartet Op. 76, No. 3. Unfortunately, the Third Reich used the melody for their own anthem, "Deutschland, Deutschland über alles."

The text is by John Newton, best remembered for "Amazing Grace." Based on the Book of Isaiah, Chap. 33, verses 20 and 21, it first appeared in *Olney Hymns* (1779). The Haydn tune was joined with the text for the first time in the 1889 edition of *Hymns Ancient and Modern*[24] (for more on John Newton, please see No. 25, "Amazing Grace").

---

[24]See *Harvard*, pps. 325-6.

No. 34: Glorious Things of Thee Are Spoken

See! the streams of living waters, springing from eternal love,
well supply thy sons and daughters and all fear of want remove.
Who can faint when such a river ever will their thirst assuage?
Grace which, like the Lord, the giver, never fails from age to age.

Blest inhabitants of Zion, washed in the Redeemer's blood!
Jesus, whom their souls rely on, makes them kings and priests to God.
'Tis his love his people raises over self to reign as kings:
and as priests, his solemn praises each for a thankful offering brings.

No. 35: Were You There?

Music: African-American Spiritual, arr. **Anthony Newman** (b. 1941)
Words: Traditional

First published in William E. Barton's *Old Plantation Hymns* in 1899, "Were You There?" is, curiously, one of the few African-American works to have entered the Episcopal hymnbook—this in spite of reports that the profile of the "average" Anglican from around the world is a single black woman in her twenties!

This hymn raises the troubling moral question for Christians, "Were you there when they crucified my Lord?" As metaphorical witnesses to the Crucifixion, do they participate in the causes of Christ's suffering, and, subsequently, in the suffering of all humankind?

The dilemma of being both the perpetrator and the victim of pain is expressed in the line that is central to all the verses: "oh, sometimes, it causes me to tremble, tremble, tremble"—tremble in sympathy with Christ's passion, tremble in shame at causing his suffering.

No. 35: Were You There?

Were you there when they cru- ci- fied my Lord? Were you there when they cru- ci- fied my Lord. Oh! Some- times it cau- ses me to trem- ble, trem- ble, trem- ble. Were you there when they cru- ci- fied my Lord?

Were you there when they nailed him to the tree? *(repeat)*
Oh! Sometimes, it causes me to tremble, tremble, tremble.
Were you there when they nailed him to the tree?

Were you there when they laid him in the tomb? *(repeat)*
Oh, sometimes, it causes me to tremble, tremble, tremble.
Were you there when they laid him in the tomb?

No. 36: O Sacred Head, Sore Wounded

Music: HERZLICH TUT MICH VERLANGEN, **Hans Leo Hassler** (1564-1612); adapt. and harm. **Johann Sebastian Bach** (1685-1750)
Words: **Paulus Gerhardt** (1607-1676); trans. **James Waddell Alexander** (1804-1859)

Hans Leo Hassler was a Lutheran, but he served as organist to the Catholic banker Octavian II Fugger of Augsburg before he became Music Director of Nuremberg and then organist to the Electoral Duke of Saxony. Greatly influenced by his travels to Italy, Hassler wrote in genres Lutheran and Catholic, in both German and Latin.[26]

This tune was originally published with a secular text, "Mein G'mut ist mir verwirret" in the *Lustgarten neuer teutscher Gesäng* (Nüremberg, 1601).

The text from which this version was translated was itself a free translation of "Salve caput cruentatum," part of a medieval devotional poem describing Christ's suffering on the cross. Originally thought to be the work of St. Bernard of Clairvaux, the founder of the Cistercian monastaries, it is now attributed to Arnulf of Louvain, abbot of Villers-en-Brabant (*c.*1240).

James Waddell Alexander was professor of ecclesiastical history at Princeton Theological Seminary and later minister of the Fifth Avenue Presbyterian Church in New York City. He published this translation of Gerhardt's text in the *Christian Lyre* in 1830.[27]

Like the chorale upon which "The Duteous Day Now Closeth" (No. 33) is based, this one is featured in Johann Sebastian Bach's *St. Matthew Passion*. Paul Simon used the same music for his song, "American Tune." Unfortunately, he gave credit to neither J.S. Bach nor Hassler for the creation and arrangement of the melody.

---

[26] See Brown, *Music in the Renaissance*, pg. 275.
[27] See *Harvard*, pps. 309-10.

No. 36: O Sacred Head, Sore Wounded

O sa- cred head sore wound- ed, with grief and shame weighed down, now scorn-ful- ly sur- round- ed with thorns thy on- ly crown how art thou pale with an- guish, with sore a- buse and scorn! How does that vis- age lan- guish which once was bright as morn!

Thy beauty, long desired, hath vanished from our sight;
thy power is all expired, and quenched the light of light.
Ah, me! for whom thou diest, hide not so far thy grace:
show me, O Love most highest, the brightness of thy face.

In thy most bitter passion my heart to share doth cry,
with thee for my salvation upon the cross to die.
Ah, keep my heart thus moved to stand thy cross beneath,
to mourn thee well-beloved, yet thank thee for thy death.

No. 37: Now Israel May Say, and That Truly

Music: Old 124th, from the *Geneva Psalter*, 1551
Words: Sts. 1 and 2: **William Whittingham**; St. 3: **Jackson Braider**

When Jean Calvin rejected the Catholic Church's demand for total obeisance to Rome, he was laying the groundwork for two movements. He was responding to Rome's disinterest in local and regional needs and concerns by reconnecting the clergy and the congregation to their native land. This was the beginning of modern nationalism.

Calvin also rejected the idolatry that permeated the Catholic Church, from its stained glass windows to the garish sensuality of its paintings and sculptures. Instead, he advocated a return to the Word as expressed in the opening of the Gospel According to St. John: "In the beginning was the Word, and the Word was with God, and the Word was God." In Calvin's scheme, the Word could be read, spoken, and heard; it could be text or music. But it was above all else the manifestation of Reason, and how the individual used Reason to understand his or her place in society. In pursuit of Reason, Calvinists and Puritans burned witches at the stake, but they also set the stage for Bacon's scientific method and Locke's rights of man.

Along with nationalism came the national hymn, though not all national hymns were created as such—Old 124th is a case in point. So-called because of its use in the *Geneva Psalter* (1551) as the accompaniment to Théodore de Bèze's paraphrase of Psalm 124 ("Or peut bien dire Israel"), Old 124th was embraced by the Nonconformist Scots as a way of identifying themselves as a chosen people and their land as a promised land.

No. 37: Now Israel May Say, and That Truly

Now Is- ra- el may say, and that tru- ly, if that the

Lord had not our cause main-tain'd; if that the Lord had

not our right sus- tain'd, when cru- el men a- gainst us furi-ous-

ly rose up in wrath, to make of us their prey.

Then certainly they had devour'd us all,
And swallow'd quick, for ought that we could deem;
Such was their rage, as we might well esteem.
And as fierce floods before them all things drown,
So had they brought our soul to death quite down.

Truly, we are Israel, everblessed Lord.
We are all your children, we believe your Word;
Our days, they pass in wonder at your ways,
O God, our King, you surpass all our praise,
Light of the dawning of our endless days.

No. 38: My Country, 'Tis of Thee

Music: America, from *Thesaurus Musicus*, 1744
Words: **Samuel French Smith** (1808-1895)

The history of "My Country, 'Tis of Thee" speaks very much of our mixed ancestry as Americans. Samuel French Smith was a Baptist minister and hymn writer who worked for the American Baptist Missionary Union. While a student at Andover Seminary in Massachusetts, Smith was asked to translate texts from several German song collections. One of the songs was "Gott segne Sachsenland," and the tune of this song inspired Smith to write the text as we know it. The hymn was first sung on 4 July, 1831.

Curiously, the tune of "Gott segne Sachsenland" was that of an English national hymn, "God save our Lord the King," first published in the English *Thesaurus Musicus*. It was later changed to "God save our gracious king," the English national anthem.

Following Charles Stuart's foiled invasion of the United Kingdom in 1745, which witnessed the last battle ever fought on British soil, both the text and tune became so popular that the song became the model—if not the actual source—for national songs in many European countries, among them Saxony. It was in light of the popularity of this song, for example, that Franz Josef Haydn was asked to compose a national anthem for Austria (see No. 34, "Glorious Things of Thee Are Spoken").[28]

[28] See *Harvard*, pg. 346.

No. 38: My Country, 'Tis of Thee

My coun-try, 'tis of thee, sweet land of lib-er-ty, of thee I sing; land where my fa-thers died, land of the pil-grim's pride, from ev-ery moun-tain-side let free-dom ring.

My native country, thee, land of the noble free,
thy name I love;
I love thy rocks and rills, thy woods and templed hills,
my heart with rapture fills
like that above.

Let music swell the breeze, and ring from all the trees
sweet freedom's song;
let mortal tongues awake, let all that breathe partake,
let rocks their silence break,
the sound prolong.

No. 39: GOD OF OUR FATHERS

Music: NATIONAL HYMN, **George William Warren** (1828-1902)
Words: **David Crane Roberts** (1841-1907)

The national hymn has two roles to play on behalf of its people. On the one hand, it captures their identity, expressing the common bonds that join these various communities together. On the other, it expresses their reason for existing as a nation.

People came to America for many different reasons: as religious and political refugees, as adventurers and entrepreneurs, as prisoners, as slaves. The first white settlers who came to America were from all parts of Europe, bringing with them a broad spectrum of attitudes and beliefs, customs, and ideals.

Given the role of the national anthem, then, it is scarcely surprising that the United States did not even have a national anthem until 1916 ("The Star-Spangled Banner"), and that spoke as much of warfare as it did of the truths that we all believe to be self-evident. Before then, numerous songs had been written to be our national anthem—among them "America the Beautiful," "The Battle Hymn of the Republic," and this hymn—but none had been chosen.

"God of Our Fathers," like "America the Beautiful," is very much about this land. For those who had come from the pestilential and densely populated Europe, America was a horizonless, verdant place, abundant in the very thing that was so profoundly craved in Europe: open territory, unpossessed and unchartered wilderness.

It was as if, for those who fled religious and political persecution, this were indeed the Promised Land. The imagery presented in this hymn speaks of the place rather than of its leaders; it speaks of America as a gift from God, whose "bounteous goodness" will "nourish us in peace."

No. 39: GOD OF OUR FATHERS

God of our fa- thers, whose al- might-y

hand lead forth in beau- ty all the star-ry band
of shin- ing worlds in splen-dor through the skies, our grate- ful

songs be- fore thy throne a- rise.

Thy love divine hath led us in the past,
in this free land by thee our lot is cast;
be thou our ruler, guardian and stay,
thy word our law, thy paths our chosen way.

From war's alarms, from deadly pestilence,
be thy strong arm our eversure defense;
thy true religion in our hearts increase,
thy bounteous goodness nourish us in peace.

No. 40: As with Gladness Men of Old

Music: Dix, melody **Conrad Kocher** (1786-1872); arr. **William Henry Monk** (1823-1889)
Words: **William Chatterton Dix** (1837-1898)

One of the more curious elements of hymnody is the way in which the same tune can be used to advantage as the accompaniment for different works. Though we have already seen the tune Dix used as the accompaniment to Anna Laetitia Barbauld's "Praise to God, Immortal Praise," the arrangement was first prepared for this text by William Chatterton Dix, the insurance manager from Glasgow—hence the name given the tune.

In its original form in *Hymns Ancient and Modern*, the tune accompanies a text intended for Epiphany, the feast celebrating the arrival of the Three Kings at the Christ Child's manger. The Barbauld text, at least in American circles, is used for a hymn generally sung at Thanksgiving.

For a history of this tune, its writer and arranger, please turn to No. 2, "Praise to God, Immortal Praise."

No. 40: As with Gladness Men of Old

As with glad-ness men of old did the guid-ing star be-hold; as with
joy they hailed its light, lead-ing on-ward, beam-ing bright; so most
gra-cious Lord, may we ev-er-more be led to thee.

As with joyful steps they sped
to that lowly mangerbed;
there to bend the knee before
him whom heaven and earth adore;
so may we with willing feet
ever seek the mercyseat.

As they offered gifts most rare
at that manger rude and bare;
so may we with holy joy,
pure and free from sin's alloy,
all our costliest treasures bring,
Christ! to thee, our heavenly King.

INDEX

THE ORDER OF THE MUSIC

1. **A Mighty Fortress Is Our God** *(2:42)*
2. **Praise to God, Immortal Praise** *(1:25)*
3. **Jesus Christ Is Risen Today** *(2:07)*
4. **The Strife Is O'er** *(1:21)*
5. **Lift Up Your Hearts** *(1:24)*
6. **Come, Ye Faithful, Raise the Strain** *(1:45)*
7. **He Is Risen! He Is Risen!** *(1:25)*
8. **Behold the King** *(2:00)*
9. **Lo! He Comes** *(1:42)*
10. **Sleepers, Awake!** *(3:49)*
11. **All Glory, Laud, and Honor** *(1:54)*
12. **The Joining of the Feast** *(1:28)*
13. **Come with Us, O Blessed Jesus** *(2:32)*
14. **Father, We Thank Thee** *(3:02)*
15. **Lord, Dismiss Us with Thy Blessing** *(2:03)*
16. **My God, Thy Table Now Is Spread** *(1:49)*
17. **Crown Him with Many Crowns** *(1:44)*
18. **Lift Up Your Heads** *(1:17)*
19. **Alleluia! Sing to Jesus!** *(2:32)*
20. **Holy God, We Praise Thy Name** *(1:54)*
21. **Come, Thou Almighty King** *(1:21)*
22. **Holy, Holy, Holy!** *(1:48)*
23. **Rock of Ages** *(1:58)*
24. **O God, Our Help in Ages Past** *(1:10)*
25. **Amazing Grace** *(1:43)*
26. **Abide with Me** *(2:08)*
27. **Joyful, Joyful, We Adore Thee** *(1:40)*
28. **God, My King, Thy Might Confessing** *(1:06)*
29. **Fairest Lord Jesus, Ruler of All Nature** *(1:49)*
30. **Now Thank We All Our God** *(1:41)*
31. **God the Omnipotent** *(1:50)*
32. **Coventry Carol** *(1:46)*
33. **The Duteous Day Now Closeth** *(2:08)*
34. **Glorious Things of Thee Are Spoken** *(2:14)*
35. **Were You There?** *(2:19)*
36. **O Sacred Head, Sore Wounded** *(2:51)*
37. **Now Israel May Say, and that Truly** *(2:23)*
38. **My Country, 'Tis of Thee** *(1:26)*
39. **God of Our Fathers** *(1:54)*
40. **As with Gladness, Men of Old** *(1:27)*

Anthony Newman: Organist and Arranger
The Chestnut Brass Company

Bruce Barrie: Trumpet
Tom Cook: Trumpet
Marian Hesse: French horn
Larry Zimmerman: Trombone
Jay Krush: Tuba
with Ben Harms: Timpani